Feelings

Jealous

Sarah Medina
Illustrated by Jo Brooker

Heinemann Library
Chicago, Illinois

Customer Service 888–454–2279
Visit our website at www.heinemannlibrary.com

Photo research by Erica Martin
Designed by Jo Malivoire
Printed in China by South China Printing Company Limited

11 10 09 08 07
10 9 8 7 6 5 4 3 2 1

Library of Congress Cataloging-in-Publication Data
Medina, Sarah, 1960-
  Jealous / Sarah Medina.
    p. cm. -- (Feelings)
  Includes bibliographical references and index.
  ISBN-13: 978-1-4034-9294-4 (hardcover)
  ISBN-10: 1-4034-9294-8 (hardcover)
  ISBN-13: 978-1-4034-9301-9 (pbk.)
  ISBN-10: 1-4034-9301-4 (pbk.)
  1. Jealousy in children--Juvenile literature. I. Title.
  BF723.J4M43 2007
  152.4'8--dc22

                          2006025129

Acknowledgments
The author and publisher are grateful to the following for permission to reproduce
copyright material: Bananastock p. **22C, D**; Corbis p. **12** (bottom), p**14, 18**; Getty Images/
photodisc p. **12** (top); Getty Images/Taxi p. **22B**; Punchstock/Photodisc p. **22A**.

Every effort has been made to contact copyright holders of any material reproduced
in this book. Any omissions will be rectified in subsequent printings if notice is given
to the publisher.

Contents

Some words are shown in bold, **like this**. They are explained in the glossary on page 23.

What Is Jealousy?

Jealousy is a **feeling**. Feelings are something you feel inside. Everyone has different feelings all the time.

happy

angry

sad

When you are jealous, you might think that other people have more than you.

What Happens When I Am Jealous?

When you are jealous, you might feel sad and **lonely**. You might not want to talk or play.

Being jealous can also make you feel angry. You might feel like saying or doing unkind things.

Why Do People Feel Jealous?

People feel jealous for all kinds of reasons. They might want something that someone else has.

Some people feel jealous of their brother or sister. They might think that the baby gets all the **attention**.

Is It Okay to Be Jealous?

Jealousy is a normal **feeling**. Everyone feels jealous sometimes.

It is not good to stay jealous for too long. It is much better to be happy for other people.

What Can I Do When I Am Jealous?

If you feel jealous, tell someone.
Talk to a parent or teacher.

Remember everything that you do well.
You might not be the best at painting,
but you could be great at making models!

13

Will I Always Feel Jealous?

All **feelings** change over time. You will not feel jealous forever.

Try being kind to the person you are jealous of. Soon you will both feel happy!

How Can I Tell If Someone Is Jealous?

People who feel jealous might seem angry. They might hurt you by saying or doing mean things.

Jealousy can make people feel sad
or **lonely**. They may not want to play
with anyone.

17

Can I Help When Someone Is Jealous?

You can help someone who is jealous. Be kind to them. Invite them to play with you.

Tell them that you like them. Then
they will know that you want to be
their friend.

I Feel Better Now!

Everyone feels jealous sometimes.
If you know what to do with jealous
feelings, they will soon pass.

Everyone is special in different ways,
and that includes you! Be happy with
yourself just as you are.

What Are
These Feelings?

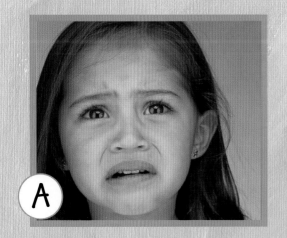

A

B

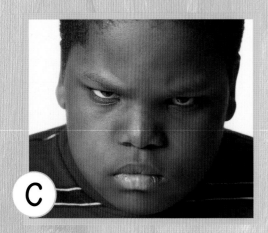

C

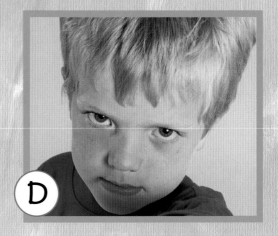

D

Which of these people look happy?

What are the other people feeling?

Look at page 24 to see the answers.

Picture Glossary

attention

when someone spends time talking to another person or doing things with them

feeling

something that you feel inside. Jealousy is a feeling.

lonely

when you feel all alone. Loneliness is a feeling.

Index

Answers to questions on page 22

The person in picture B looks happy. The other people could be sad, angry, or lonely.

Note to Parents and Teachers

Reading for information is an important part of a child's literacy development. Learning begins with a question about something. Help children think of themselves as investigators and researchers by encouraging their questions about the world around them. Most chapters in this book begin with a question. Read the question together. Look at the pictures. Talk about what you think the answer might be. Then read the text to find out if your predictions were correct. Think of other questions you could ask about the topic, and discuss where you might find the answers. Assist children in using the picture glossary and the index to practice new vocabulary and research skills.